WILDTRACK

WILDTRACK

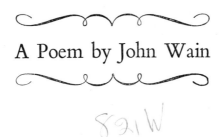

A Poem by John Wain

821 W

MACMILLAN
London · Melbourne · Toronto
1965

MACMILLAN AND COMPANY LIMITED
Little Essex Street London WC 2
also Bombay Calcutta Madras Melbourne

THE MACMILLAN COMPANY OF CANADA LIMITED
70 Bond Street Toronto 2

PRINTED IN GREAT BRITAIN

TO MY SONS

Possess, as I possessed a season,
The countries I resign

During the course of composition, extracts from this poem appeared in *The Critical Quarterly* (Hull, England) and *The Carleton Miscellany* (Minnesota, U.S.A.), whose editors are thanked for permission to reprint.

The descent of the Occidental sciences from the heavens to the earth (from 17th-century astronomy to 19th-century biology), and their concentration to-day, at last, on man himself (in 20th-century anthropology and psychology), mark the path of a prodigious transfer of the focal point of human wonder. Not the animal world, not the plant world, not the miracle of the spheres, but man himself is now the crucial mystery. Man is that alien presence with whom the forces of egoism must come to terms, through whom the ego is to be crucified and resurrected, and in whose image society is to be reformed.

JOSEPH CAMPBELL, *The Hero with a Thousand Faces*

Engrave the snowflake. But without hindering its downward
dance. Carve your biography in images,
one for each flake, and take as many
flakes as you need. But (this is your legendary
task) never hold one in your hand. The warm
touch of human skin melts them to water. (As
the man said, one's name cannot be written
there.) Engrave an image on each tumbling
weightless flake. Above, the opaque grey
future: underfoot, the trodden slush
of the past (dog-pee and fag-end speckle
an outline of geological dignity).
Only the falling snowflake is the Now.

To write of the Now on the down-drifting
frozen angel-feather of This, the revolving
snowflake in its carelessness of before
and after, to engrave particular facts,
specific adventures of eye and finger-tip,
and always with no break in the resigned
eager dance of the snowflakes, their sift and winnow:
this is your task:

BEGIN

I think of January 1918
the Germans breaking through on the Western
Front BAM BAM WHEEEEE CRUMP and in
Moscow and Petersburg snow falling
and civil war BAM BAM. Snow
seen by Alexander Blok
lifted in spirals by the wind
Alexander Blok watching the snow
four January days. Engraving
world history, the history of Russian
heartbeats on unmelting

I

snowflakes despite BAM BAM. Crumple
of corpses soon to stiffen. Blok
graved with a diamond his nation's
heartbeats on twelve snowflakes.

Twelve snowflakes sifted down:
and a few more followed, partners
without volition. Only Blok
with one thin graving tool could image
January 1918 on twelve snowflakes
plus the odd few for luck.

I see that snow on the pavements
trampled into a paste with mud and spittle
I feel that wind
a man could lean against that wind
no overcoat
for the poor old woman who
looks up and reads
the banner strung between the houses

ALL POWER TO THE CONSTITUENT ASSEMBLY

Holy Mother of God she says

what a waste
all that cloth

And here come the Twelve
cracked boots and frayed rifle-slings
but e rifles in working order
ready for BAM BAM BAM

Twelve snowflakes caressed in midfall
by the cool fingertip
and the bright diamond
of Alexander Blok

Twelve snowflakes sifting down
and the odd few for luck

Vanya and Katya taking a sleigh-ride
Vanya the out-smarter
always with it Vanya
never misses a trick
and Katya
the officers' whore
with her stockings wedged full
of currency notes

Notes issued by the Kerensky government
yes that same Kerensky
who walked the other night
down the road near the house
where I John Wain sit writing this
in Oxford, England
Kerensky
himself a snowflake
still winnowing down
an old man with memories

Katya you officers' whore
you are wanted
wanted by the Twelve
a private has one too Katya
a worker, a man with empty pockets
has one too
it's time you tried it Katya
up to the neck you bitch

BAM BAM and the coachman
whips up his horses
Vanya gets away as usual
but Katya lies still

You bought it Katya
the Kerenkas in your stockings
paid for it
A snowflake Katya
                    trampled
                              underfoot

3

Twelve snowflakes sifting down
and the odd few for luck.

Then the bourgeois
O God yes the bourgeois
he stands on the corner with his fur
collar turned up and his mangy
bow-wow beside him

His collar is turned up so far
only the tip of his nose
sticks out

We needn't feel sorry for him
any more
a snowflake settles on the tip of his nose
a falling snowflake
lost
like Katya
yes we feel sorry for Katya
but not for the bourgeois on the corner
BAM BAM BAM
he sucked our blood long enough
and you dog scoot
scuttle away
                    you hear?

But he follows
tail down. Old Russia
is dead. Old Russian ways
are dead and here come
the Twelve leaning against the wind
stumping in the snow
one lags behind
thinking of Katya
a dead piece of free-market
luxury with a sweet birthmark

4

on her shoulder but never mind
the dog's tail is well down
Old Russia must die BAM
BAM

Alexander Blok with his face pressed to the pane
saw twelve snowflakes fall that can never fall again

Clumsy cracked boots stamped through the spiralling snow
the Twelve were marching the way they had to go

their history was already written, they had no choice
only the dog howled, only the old woman's voice

came to Alexander Blok's ear as he gazed down
from his unsleeping window and saw the town

the streets the markets the canals and the faces
upturned to the pitiless snowstorm that left no traces

of the beggar's spittle or the bourgeois' terrified eyes
or the Kerenkas wedged in the warmth of Katya's thighs

Speak to me tense poet from your visionary gloom
say why you leave your chair and pace about your room

confess Alexander Blok confess what you see
as the twelve march straight ahead singing softly

Confess that your eyes grow wide and your reason rambles
as you smell the hot blood from the human shambles

when the Twelve shall break open the vials of their wrath
and pity like that starved cur be kicked from their path

Confess Alexander Blok that you hear the screams
of children at night dragged from the warmth of their dreams

running to hide in alleys full of demented figures
running blindly as the Twelve press their steel triggers

You who see Jesus Christ at the head of the Twelve
is it the wounds of humanity he comes to salve

or is it not rather a new furnace he prepares
for the flesh that only in death lays down its cares

is it not rather the mighty embrace of death
he has ready for these creatures of blood and breath

Blok you foresee the hour that must come to birth
when you will cry 'the woodlouse has inherited the earth'

These will be the years of the mindless gnawing louse
when central and eastern Europe is one huge torture-house

when the Rhine and the Moskva flow between aching walls
and the sky is empty where the human victim calls

You Alexander Blok foresee this in your agony
and you are right to see Jesus Christ who cannot die

Leading the Twelve into those years of crucifixion
for Christ walks on earth only in one direction

it is always towards the blood-soaked Cross that he moves
to the sound of distant trumpets and approaching hooves

for Christ's way forward lies through the gates of pain
and he has come to be crucified again

with the children hiding in the alleys and the shivering brutes
who were men until the Twelve began to shoot

but when they heard the guns went down on hands and knees
and chewed bitter grass under the leafless trees

Confess confess Blok you see the children's eyes
as dry and empty as the unpitying skies

the cell doors will slam, the soldiers will strut like geese
Christ will be crucified by the secret police

and to see the white streak of hope beyond this night
is beyond the reach of your pale dilated sight

you will sink without hope into silence and neglect
and your world be left to the mad dog and the insect

your window will be blank above the windy square
when your eyes have closed with weariness and despair

and yet despair is not the end, Blok your voice will sound
when the Twelve you loved lie deep in the frozen ground

for you watched them move forward against the mocking wind
you saw the tattered cloth of revolt that they pinned

over their naked flesh in that freezing air
you saw their harsh humanity as they laughed and swore

and as you watched the Twelve marching with iron feet
you loved them, you longed for sheaves of golden wheat

ripe fruits and flowers to toss on the hard stone
that the Twelve might have something they could call their own

beyond the frown of vengeance and the doubled fist
and so you saw dimly in the freezing mist

the figure of Jesus Christ arisen from his sleep
leading the twelve like shepherds to the hungry sheep

this was your vision on the night of the black sky
and I honour you Alexander Blok with your dilated eye

you felt the hunger of those lost and homeless crowds
and your pity called down Christ from above the clouds:

I feel it too, mindless as the falling snow
that prints its ironic kiss on the white faces below

I see the faces upturned amid the unceasing snowflakes
and I see the poet who weeps and aches

seeing already the world of the woodlouse-state
in which the cry of the living man will come too late

longing to walk with the twelve, to share their load
yet fearing the eyeless walls which line that road

fearing the dead bricks and the soundproof air
where the footsteps of the Twelve echo only despair

confess Alexander Blok you fear those walls
between which the twelve go forward like doomed animals

and the figure of Christ dwindles to a scarf of mist
and becomes again the pale Christ whom Judas kissed!

a man walks out alone
his two feet sucking
like a fly's feet at the tilted earth
alone
save for the other within his skin
always that other
hidden from him, yet present
meaningful,
           qualifying,
                  expert in *nuance*.
In the broad shaft of the sun
the man alone throws a shadow

In the dark sea of sleep
someone beside him stirs the fine sand

fish dart questioningly
birds peer from the trees

always that other
stays close

Je est un autre!

The day-self moves in a broad shaft
The night-self is secret and daft

The day-self joins with eager others.
The night-self has no friends, only brothers.

The day-self is poltroon or hero :
The night-self is picaro, pierrot.

The day-self can choose to tell lies.
The night-self speaks truth, or he dies.

ADVENTURES OF THE DAY-SELF
IN THE AGE OF THE MACHINES

The wheels turn. 'History is bunk.' Homogenize!
Identical objects spooling from a band.
Ford's little jokes : any colour, so long
as it's black. The cold grin
makes taste a whim, and memory an encumbrance.
In the Ford Museum, at Detroit, they have
no record of Ford's original techniques.
This is Chronos devouring his sons. The last maker
of history swallows all previous history down.

How they
hated him, the clever ones!

How they
wanted to kick back and hurt!

Henry Ford,
who threatened all they lived by,
with his long spanner and his hard contempt.

Aldous Huxley
put him in the centre of *Brave New World*
like Dante putting people into Hell.

C. S. Lewis
bluffly called him 'an ignorant mechanic'.

Edmund Wilson
blew the gaff on Henry's little game.

When the market for his cars was booming and his payroll was at its thickest,
he used often to drop into his factories and chat with his employees; he is said to-
day never to visit them unaccompanied by a guard of twenty men.
                                                    The American Earthquake

How they hated him,
minds to whom the past was rich with meaning!

And yet, why should he care about the past?
Nothing occurred in Dearborn, Michigan,
where he was born, till locomotives ran.
Before that, weather. And the skies were vast.

Nothing but motion could seem important there,
where men and cattle had been frozen down
so many winters, and the roofs of town
sweated all summer in the stagnant air.

Legs were no use in that enormous plain.
Only the wheel could make dead Dearborn live.
He dreamed of wheels as sailors dream of girls.

Cars were his logic. Who can own a train?
The wind of the great roads was his to give,
and petrol pumps as elegant as pearls!

Henry is my darling,
          my darling,
          my darling,
Henry is my darling,
And I'm his Model T.

I'll let him devise me,
          revise me,
          disguise me,
And I'll let him surprise me,
For I'm his Model T.

I'll let him lay me on his line
And standardize each part:
I'll double his production with
The love that's in my heart:

O, Henry is my new man,
          my true man,
          my glue man,

He's my much ado man,
He's my black and blue man,
He's my cockatoo man,
And I'm his Model T!

The only enemy is the earth itself,
the flat, dusty earth of which God made too much.
The only ally, motion.

Move!

Keep those

men and materials rolling, always rolling!

Those colonels with their moustaches and their manners,
those coal-black mammies, all the unseen throats
that poured free music out on the enslaved air,
those naked feet slapping the naked earth,

why, all they needed was the Model T!
Swing low, sweet Model T, was what they meant!

Yankees, you should have waited.   Henry was coming.
The red badge of courage was bunk like all the rest.
A radiator badge would have done the job.

This is	the dance of mass-production
weaving	the pattern of the future
treading	the past into oblivion
fingers	of immigrant and native
muscles	of german and italian
polish	and jewish eyes in focus
sinews	of negro and armenian
dancing	the dance of mass-production
speeding	components on to wholeness
engines	to couple with transmission
gearbox	and tyres and rims uniting
building	the Model-T together
making	the one out of the many
speaking	the language of to-morrow
grammar	of time and motion study
syntax	of orchestrated effort

WHERE NOW   IS HISTORY THE OGRE?

faded   like the moonlight in the morning
still there   but faded in the morning

History had nailed Dearborn to the earth,
the flat dusty earth of which God made too much.
And so, the boy from Dearborn broke it up,
plucked up nailed Dearborn, mounted it on wheels,
started America moving.
                    Frontiers,
where ideas tear each other's bellies out,
That's history. We get dragged in too. So what?
This is the last time round. History is dead,
now no one has to stay in the same place
from birth to death, now common men can move,
roll up this dusty earth which held them apart
and gave them different languages and names.

The Model T is born. History dies.
Fortunate boys and girls, homogenize!

Meanwhile, back at the ranch-house :
                    the good old
Russian and Ukrainian ranch-house, the fight is on.

Sped down the line from Moscow, the decisions
of hard-eyed men in offices become
the talk of villagers whose mouths are dry.
The peasants cluster round the notice-boards.
Josef Vassarionovich Dzhugashvili
is giving the orders : and they turn out to be
the same as Henry Ford's : homogenize!

Twenty-five million peasant holdings must
be crunched together into one flat shape :
the shape of the future, the immense kolkhoz.

The kulaks have refused to collectivize.

Question time.   Raise your right hand and swear.

Who is Vassarionovich Dzhugashvili ?
The man in the Kremlin.   He gives the orders.

Why do the peasants wish to oppose his will ?
Instinctively they fear the great machine.

What will he do when they oppose his will ?
He will destroy them.   Five million will die,
the rest will live in slavery and fear.

How will the five million die ?
                         Of hunger.   When
they have killed their beasts and left their grain to rot.
These actions are their gesture.   Now they wait.

Do they expect to die ?
                    No.   They believe
no ruler would let so many people starve.

And what does Vassarionovich Dzhugashvili say ?
He gives them leave to lie in their huts and die.

Has he no mercy, this Vassarionovich?
He has invented a nature for himself.
He has abandoned his limpid Georgian name
and commanded that they call him *Stalin*, steel.

Have the peasants, then, no chance?
                              No chance at all.
It is the nature of steel to beat them down:
it is the nature of steel to chew their flesh,
to flatten them, to cut them into shapes
that can be fitted to the great machine.

(*Hymn to Steel:*
for 5 million human voices)

    Great cutting edge,
       indifferent to tissue
    Great stamping mass,
       indifferent to the cry of crushed bones,
    Grant us your hardness:
    We would be as prompt to suffer
    As you to inflict our suffering!

    Light flashes out
       from your whirling blades
    Heads bow to the earth
       before your harvesting:
    Heads of grain, heads of men and women.
    Grant us your hardness and bright surface.

    Be with us in the hour of our processing.

    In you is our strength
       therefore destroy us
    In you is our hope
       therefore destroy us
    From you we have the unanswerable word
    that we have become our own enemies

if our enemies live we must surely perish
therefore destroy us.

Bite through the soft tendons of our children
Bite through the dried flesh of our elders :
Drink the strength of our men
the fertility of our women
and stamp all tears into the mud.

This we ask
in the sacred name
the surgical, liturgical name
(ever to be praised by the dazed
ever to be acclaimed by the maimed
unceasingly to be said by the dead)
name
of
STEEL

I believe that the fundamental need of the Russian soul is a thirst for suffering, a
constant thirst in everything and from all time.

Dostoievsky, *Diary of an Author*

Five million die. The rest homogenize.

*(lament of the
Homogenized Man)*

The moon swings low over the white fields.
Irresolute I stand, a black full stop
in her calm discourse.

I turn to walk back to the dusty street.
My shadow lopes like a wolf
The night hates me.

I want to apologize to the cool grass.
Something is ticking in my ears:
It is my metal heart.

Khasan Israelov, dead in an unknown grave,
I speak in a voice that wishes it were yours.

The Chechen-Ingush, a mountain people in the northern Caucasus, resisted
domination by Catherine the Great of Russia, and were not finally subdued till
1859; they revolted against the Czars in 1867, 1877 and 1905, and after the Soviets
came to power they continued to resist absorption and collectivization. They
rebelled in 1930, and were crushed. In 1941, the Chechen-Ingush struck for
their freedom one last time, under the leadership of a young poet, Khasan Israelov. Stalin's answer was to obliterate the entire nation by execution and mass
deportation on February 23, 1944. Under the direction of General Serov, the
entire operation, whereby 500,000 people were swept off to death or slavery,
took just twenty-four hours.

1.

All those who knew you are dispersed or dead
five hundred thousand people wiped away
corpses or prisoners to the last one.
But listen, Khasan Israelov, where you lie.
I speak in a voice that wishes it were yours.
Listen, Khasan, with your mud-stopped ear.

2.

I saw your mountains once, not far away.
In the cold Caucasus I saw them lie
as the eagle sees them, high-shining, one by one.
They know you, Khasan, still, though you are dead.
The wind whose tunes put magic in your ear
whirls in the crannies where the wild goats lie.

3.

Eryri or Wicklow, half a world away
I tread on hill-paths that were never yours
and pluck the fragrant heather where I lie.
Mountains are many, but their voice is one,
still crying freedom! in the world's ear,
though by each bluff stiffen the defiant dead.

4.

Climb with me, Khasan, till bitterness is dead.
I have not the strength to face an end like yours.
But take this homage, do not turn away.

I hear your mountain music, though my ear
is dulled with cowardice: you are the one
to guide me where the quiet heroes lie.

5.

Khasan, your written chronicle is a brief one.
Such sagas are banned from the captive ear.
Soldiers have killed, how bureaucrats must lie.
Five hundred thousand truths to sponge away.
If your name lives, the victory will be yours.
Your strength cannot be tamed now you are dead.

6.

The wild chamois is your symbol, if you need one:
Who, chased to the final edge where the hunt stops dead,
Leaps down, with a delicate madness much like yours.
May its gentle ghost be welcome where your bones lie,
Who thought rather to throw life steeply away
Than make a story pleasant to the huntsman's ear!

Khasan, only courage like yours can burn hatred away.
Unstop your ear: pity me from where you lie:
Climb with me, turbulent one, till bitterness is dead!

(*Homage to the
Irreducible I*)

Under eternal house arrest, the dissenter
Calmly preserving the verities from decay
Has made his home in the impregnable centre.

Watched by police who never move away
who remain alert and in touch with headquarters
at his ironic window he sits all day.

Threatened with tear-gas, badgered by reporters
waiting to photograph his leap to suicide,
he listens to the surf of distant waters,

observes the sky where clouds bunch and divide,
idly notes the numbers of passing cars:
the truly proud one who never thinks of pride.

18

His name occurs in hushed dialogues in bars.
The police order him through megaphones to come down.
He receives code messages from the outer stars.

His house is magic.   The staircase dissolves in splinters
at the touch of a trooper's foot.   His front door
is cemented up.   Hence no visitor enters,

yet voices laughing and singing, and what is more
inexplicable, feminine sounds of pleasure
can often be heard.   Gift-bundles for the poor

parachute from his window, or sway at leisure
from coloured balloons which patiently deflate,
lowering to children's hands their holiday treasure.

No wonder the chief of police has to work late.
If they try to dismantle the house, its bewildering walls
turn to mist.   Then resume at will their firmness and weight.

So the man never comes down and the house never falls.

(*Attitude of Humanity
towards the Irreducible I*)

They pin their faith
entirely on this indestructible wraith

who, ages upon ages,
has coolly survived the fury of outrages.

In the stone pinnacle
of the fortress they construct from dream and miracle

tangible and assertive,
he comforts those whose happiness is abortive.

Knight without armour,
high chanticleer, spirit's alarmer,

secret soothsayer,
he reveals the strategies of Time the betrayer.

19

Because he is one,
his children and lovers are never entirely alone :

because he is single
their multiple faces are free to shuttle and mingle.

he asks no prayers :
he fulfills his own nature in fulfilling theirs.

His terms are simple :
he has no metaphysical crust and no temple.

He is part of creation :
a figure, like us, in God's difficult equation.

We know him well, there is no need to prove him.
Our cold curses follow those who would remove him.
We are still human while none is set above him.
Therefore,
                we love him.

So sang, briefly in unison,
night-self and day-self. Choosing
to be human in all they concur in.
Meanwhile, back at the bone-house :

ADVENTURES OF THE NIGHT-SELF
IN THE AGE OF THE MACHINES

(*Sonnet:*
Feigned to be spoken by
the Maniac among the Tombs —
St. Mark, Chapter 5)

If now I roar, and gash myself with stones,
it is to draw him to the fight. I hoard
in these mad cells those that must call him lord.
I tempt the fiends to pasture in these bones.

Two thousand beasts could not contain my sins.
Not one but many devils claw my sides.
It is my ribs the foul night-hag bestrides,
through whose dry lips all lust and hatred grins.

Because my name is Legion, and my brain
is swarming with the maggots of despair,
he hears the trumpet of my sufferings:

they will do battle on this narrow plain.
Already, through the dark death-smelling air,
I hear the clapping of their furious wings.

See now,
the reverent burlesques begin.

Man worships by parody.
The outward miracles of Christ, the inward miracles of the Buddha:
on the fourth day, the noose and the two razors.

If Christ's touch could heal, Christ's spittle mix with dust
to make new tissue, plastic surgery
performed with the spit glands only, why then!

men who were near to heaven could channel down
the healing energies of Christ. And who
was nearer to heaven than a saintly king?

Malcolm   Comes the King forth I pray you?

Doctor   I sir: there are a crew of wretched Soules
That stay his Cure: their malady convinces
The great assay of Art. But at his touch,
Such sanctity hath Heauen giuen his hand,
They presently amend.

                    Worship by parody!
Crazed with their sufferings, skeletal or bloated
arms raised to pull down mercy on their matted heads,
the sick jostle and crane. Will the king come? Will
the anointed palm press on this aching flesh?

Theirs is a sweating faith. A crew of wretched Soules.
Bless thy people. Will the king come? His touch bind up
the rents and pockholes in their pitiful skin?

On the fourth day, the noose and the two razors.

Bless thy people. Bless thy people. Rolled
in the dirt by a conqueror they never challenged,
poison-splashed, stamped on by unseen boots,
they hold up their hands to majesty, not their eyes.
In the bright face of heaven they dare not look.

The king is their best magic.

It is a fundamental article of the Shilluk creed that the spirit of the divine or
semi-divine Nyakang is incarnate in the reigning king, who is accordingly himself invested to some extent with the character of a divinity. But while the
Shilluk hold their kings in high, indeed religious reverence and take every
precaution against their accidental death, nevertheless they cherish 'the con-
viction that the king must not be allowed to become ill or senile, lest with his
diminishing vigour the cattle should sicken and fail to bear their increase, the
crops should rot in the fields, and man, stricken with disease, would die in
ever-increasing numbers.' To prevent these calamities it used to be the regular
custom with the Shilluk to put the king to death whenever he showed signs of
ill-health or failing strength.   Frazer, *The Golden Bough*, XXIV

                    Do not feare our person:
There's such Diuinity doth hedge a King,
That Treason can but peepe to what it would,
Acts little of his will.
                    But what is treason?
To the king's body, or to the king's soul?
The piety of the Shilluk teaches how
to disregard the flesh. If the king's soul leaks out
through mouth or nostril, it wanders unattended.
A sorcerer might trick and imprison it. And even
without sorcerers, how can the people be sure
the soul that keeps them safe will be transferred
to the rightful body of the king's successor?

In some tribes of Fazoql the king had to administer justice daily under a certain
tree. If from sickness or any other cause he was unable to discharge this duty
for three whole days, he was hanged on the tree in a noose, which contained

two razors so arranged that when the noose was drawn tight by the weight of the king's body they cut his throat. *Frazer, ibid.*

On the fourth day, the noose and the two razors.

Primitives, of course. The seventeenth century
looking back on the tenth. Edwardian Cambridge
comparing the field notes of anthropologists.

It is said that Frazer was allowed
to keep his Cambridge fellowship just so long
as he drew no conclusions from his evidence.

On the fourth day, the noose and the two razors.

So here, dry reeds swayed by the wind of hope,
the sick jostle and crane outside the palace.
Mediaeval devotion. A burning, half-shut eye.
Did the scrofulous
never recover? Did no healed man
skip home to his village in the fens or mountains
shouting the evidence of a miracle?
Miracles have no evidence. The Age
of Reason was not reasonable.
                              Dr. Swinfen
made important discoveries about the
circulation of the blood: a true
eighteenth-century empiricist he. Yet
when the tears ran down
Sarah Johnson's face
(bookseller's wife, forty-two
years old, her large pale child
variously afflicted)
                              the tears ran down
and Dr. Swinfen said:
'Take the child to London,
                              to the Queen.'
Why? from belief? or
because of the tears on her
poor plain cheeks?
Sam Johnson:

thirty months old, and like
to die. His arm
suppurates. They keep it open
with a knife. Further,
Dr. Swinfen diagnoses
scrofula.
The tears run down.
                    Bless thy people!
Scrofula is tuberculosis of the lymph glands.
Touch little crying Sam with royal fingers.

March, 1712. The coach
grinds down from Lichfield. Damp-faced Sam
is sick. The other passengers
complain. Human misery
never changes. A crew of wretched Soules
that stay his Cure.

'What do you remember?'
                              'An old lady in black,
wearing diamonds.'
                    What should he remember?
The royal soul was safe within her body.
Faith surged in that March morning like a river.

Gently, Sarah, lift your son
(Thirty months old, and like to die)
To where the springs of pity run:
Her pale hand on his paler face
Transmits an ancient dogged grace
Illumined by her royal eye.

An ancient dogged grace still lives
In faith that flowers out of pain.
Here God still judges and forgives.
Gently, Sarah, lift your child
Pain and sadness have defiled:
Bathe him in that magic rain.

London is huge, and we are small
(Thirty months old, and wilting fast):
Is death the dark that curtains all?
Michael is old: my loins grow dry:
Sweet Jesus, let our Sam not die!
Make London's clouds rain joy at last!

Do not speak: she knows your fear.
Her charity brims cool and fresh.
Love and pity brought you here.
Let the Lichfield women know
Sarah's child will live and grow:
Love and pity healed his flesh

And he will rule in Reason's town
In future years: yet in his brain
Some saving root will channel down
To where the springs of pity flow:
Some images will live and know
Deep within the human grain.

So this child's inheritance
(Thirty months old, and not to die)
Shall be to know the secret dance
Of dream and reason, day and night:
And with his bookish urban sight
To read the language of the sky.

We came thither too late to see what we expected, a people of peculiar appear-
ance, and a system of antiquated life. The clans retain little of their original
character . . . a longer journey than to the Highlands must be taken by him
whose curiosity pants for savage virtues and barbarous grandeur.
                    Johnson, *A Journey to the Western Islands*
                                  of Scotland, 1775.

What drew him to the Hebrides? And why
did he so question those with second sight?
Was he not satisfied with Reason's light,
who made his home beneath a city sky?

It was the approach of death that whipped his mind.
A man may cry to heaven and still burn.

His brain grasped out for something still to learn.
These islanders the world had left behind:

had they perhaps a wisdom, handed on
through blood and custom? His old bones were sore,
but through the autumn weather he must ride,

still hoping to be touched and healed once more.
Too late, too late! That ancient world was gone:
progressive Boswell chattered by his side.

Theirs was the century of madness, the lid screwed tight:
the stately wig,
                lice clinging on the scalp:
the great controlled art, a shout from under the stairs.
'And China's earth receives the smoking tide'
poised in the balance of a pirouette
above that other smoking tide of blood.

These were not prudes. Their sombre art
searched that darkness to its heart.

But their dignity and grace
combed agony, and washed its face.

Mozart and Fragonard ignore
the breath of the gin-sleeping whore.

Gulliver never travelled where
the London sewers stun the air.

Their general names for evil
masked every actual devil.

The balance is difficult. The classic portico
slips sideways into the mud.
                        There is
so much that must be stamped down out of sight.
The heavy pillars are only just heavy enough.
Soon it will come. Everyone knows that.
The signs are everywhere. Wild stories are
taken as gospel. The swell of groans

and curses drowns couplet and epigram.
This civilization is not single enough.

Just over against the Muse Gate at Charing-cross is to be seen these Rarities
following, viz. a little Man 3 Foot high, and 32 years of Age, strait and pro-
portionable every way. The next is his Wife, a little Woman, not 3 Foot high,
and 30 Years of Age, who diverts the Company by her extraordinary Dancing,
and is now big with Child, being the least Woman that ever was with Child in
Europe: Likewise their little Horse, 2 Foot odd Inches high, which performs
several wonderful Actions by the word of Command, being so small that it's
kept in a Box.   Advertisement in *The Spectator*, Thursday,
                                  December 13, 1711.

(The Little Woman
addresses the Child
in her Womb)

Lie easy in your secret cradle,
my little master.
They come to gape at this small rounded belly,
to judge and grin, to widen yokel eyes
or, oafish, taint the air with filthy jests.

'The least woman that ever was with child.'
Does God work miracles in idleness?
Their minds are sealed in large stupidity.
Their eyes are set too far above the ground.

They cannot guess your secret,
little emperor, my secret master. Lie
at anchor in your estuary there.

So many meaty hands upon the rail,
such staring … sometimes I have to pity them.
Cast out, disowned, the wrong shape for their size.
Only the cattle should lumber and bellow. Men
were meant in the Creator's mind to be
compact, neat, delicate.
                         I think of cats,
conies, and hedgehogs, in the safe embrace
of our companionable earth.

27

These oafs have huge noses.
They cannot move with the right human grace.
Sometimes I swear I have to pity them.

Lie easy there,
my hidden conqueror. Grow
through all your comely stages:
                                        first
the size of a sleek mouse: later, the size
of a bright-singing thrush.
                              Then out, and suck
from these two nipples the milk of our new day!

They pay to stare. It is an idle sport.
If they could know I hold their future here!
My little lord shall drive them howling out.
Already rumours are abroad among them —
a crazed parson has wandered to a country
which he calls Lilliput.
                              Across the seas
are many islands where our people thrive.
It must be so. The parson would not lie.
Their swords flash quick to snip through heavy sinews.
The human-beasts will topple to the earth.
Our cannon will fire too fast for them to count
the shocks that crack their bones.
                                        All we have lacked
till now, is our true leader.

                              Madness stalks them.
They cannot keep away from raree-shows.
Curiosity is their illness. To see an oddity
they travel stony miles. This is a sign
they draw towards their end. Blood drowns their sun.

Little prince, this hard world's next emperor,
I have not told your father all my thoughts.
He is a good man, but with specks of blindness.
He does not hate the human-beasts: has friends

among them : says they have done fine things.
Fine things! I feel your scorn laugh in my bones.
All that they make is wrong : too high, too thick.
Their finest houses thrust above the trees,
instead of finding shelter, as they should,
beneath those steady arms. Their music roars
as if in pain. Their cups are chamber-pots.

I do not trust your father with our secret.
One day he will share our happiness. Till then
only one heart beats with this prophecy :
the heart whose thud keeps our two beings warm.

Lie easy in your secret cradle,
my love, my rescuer,
mine and the world's new master :
God does not work His miracles in vain!

It is recorded that Dean Swift was only known to laugh twice in his life: once
when reading Fielding's *Tom Thumb*, and once when watching a juggler.

(*Sonnet: Dean Swift
contemplates the
little Woman*)

Maddened by loneliness, a Sybil's heart
in a small animal, shown to boors for pence,
her life one long affront, she draws apart
and in her prayers bulks out their penitence.

Frog-legs kick, moth-wings flutter in her womb.
Deceived by pain, she dreams enormous things :
a gnat's thin trumpet is the blast of doom :
she will be mother to a line of kings.

Her agony is mine, though not her dreams.
My fabled Lilliput was England's truth.
In bitter Ireland now I shun men's sight.

But eyes like hers, where holy hatred gleams
I welcome still : we share one sharp delight,
I in my deanery, she in her booth.

29

The voice comes
out of an emptiness.   Night-self and day-self
find here no habitable planet.

For :

belief in magic keeps
humanity from devouring its
own entrails.

Swift went
mad because he saw too clearly
where dreams end and wakefulness
begins.

In a healing dream
the lady in black touched Sam's face.
He lived.   Shilluk and Fozoql
panoplied their kings in love and
death.   Their dream
in the frightening jungle
was no different from that licensed
by Dr. Swinfen.

Night-self and day-self!
The ribboned ceremony and the dark
creaturely sty of sleep,
where motives are littered and
tug at the ranged nipples in the mud!

To have a king is to say :
We will dream of a magic person, and
when we wake that person shall
still, by our will, be magic.

Dean Swift,
You never understood!

*(Sonnet: Rousseau outside
the Gates of Geneva)*

The punctual Genevese had rung the bells,
Waited the allotted time, then closed the gate.
He stared. The walls stared back. Their solid weight
Pressed on his mind. He must be someone else:

It was too difficult to be Jean-Jacques,
Apprentice, of Geneva. But what name,
What nature could be his? A sudden shame
Clung to his shoulders like a heavy pack.

A moment, and the hesitation passed.
Reckless, a sun flared out behind his eyes,
And by its light he saw the coming age,
People with serious monsters. Lone, aghast,
He watched them rearing, heard their first blind cries:
Then turned, and started on his pilgrimage.

In France, the magic did not hold.
Above a choppy sea of gazers
King Louis bowed his head. It rolled.
This was the noose and the two razors.

Guillotine shaved the anointed head:
The single rivet had shaken loose.
'We are all statesmen', Robespierre said.
This was the two razors and the noose.

*(Sonnet: feigned to be spoken
by the Witch of Endor — Samuel, I, xxviii)*

Great kings are strong. I am alone, and old.
And yet they creep to me at night, disguised.
Death they can bear, but not to be surprised:
and stubborn ghosts ignore their blood and gold.

King Saul resents the present like a cage.
I gave my being to this cruel art

for the same reason, long ago.   My heart
was flaring with the same forbidden rage.

Altar and priest have failed.   My magic brings
stern Samuel to break his holy sleep.
Saul, God is your enemy.   You are to die.

This Saul was merciful.   Now see him weep.
He finds no pardon, who could not satisfy
the vengeful hunger of the King of Kings.

THE DAY-SELF CONTEMPLATES
THE DEFEAT OF TIME

In the rain-forest I found, the air is quiet.
Still pools collect at the feet of the great trunks:
moss grows in the green silence, creepers stir
in a breeze too faint for a girl's cheek to feel.
There, nothing dies.
                        What is discarded sinks
and pulses alluvial, feeding the deep roots.
Daylight is filtered here, and darkness lit
by phosphorescence. The presence of the forest
never sleeps, nor ever quite awakes.

To move in the forest I discard flesh.
Only the mind has passport here, for time
is cruel to the body, tolerating
only that shudder of loin on loin that brings
futurity in the endless line of births.

No flesh can walk in the forest. The still air
blows easily into the porous cells of thought
and only thought.
                        I moved among the trunks
and heavy stems, I heard the dripping leaves
conversing with the moss, and the thick stems
of rubbery marsh-plants eased to let me pass.

I went along the path that was no path
and the forest took me, silent, welcoming:
and as my vision opened in the gloom
of that green stillness, I saw others there.
Calm, solitary shapes resting among the leaves
or standing by the always-motionless trunks,
they disregarded me and each other.

What
had made them free of this primeval peace?
How had they left their flesh, that prey of time,
and come unhampered under these colonnades?

And then I saw that none was empty-handed.

Each held, like a prize too joyous to put down,
the thing that he had made.   Only this magic
was strong enough to lull the wrath of time,
and bring each maker into his fulfilment, here,
under the inexhaustibly fertile boughs.

Who first coiled springs?   Fashioned a stirrup, or
thought of a book which opened on a hinge?
Drew sounds from wood and string, or named a bird?
His liberated self was here.

I trod
the unmapped forest, marvelling, and not
I only, but others among living men:
the thoughtful-eyed, those able for an hour
to turn from the highway of the Here and Now,
leaving the flesh to cool itself awhile,
and wander for their delight in the quiet shade,
meeting now this achievement, and now that:
all turbulent minds now quiet, all fulfilled
in joyous contemplation: how this one had
designed a palace, that one distilled a drug
that could heal pain, another found a sea,
a fourth made fables that enriched men's lives.

All marvelled, and I marvelled with the rest:
but none stayed long: the calm of the great forest
could not be borne by those whose flesh was warm
and cried its hungers and its urgencies,
calling them back with swift and bitter cries:
summoned, they hurried off, and others came,
but scampered in their turn: and I, like them,
feeling my respite at an end, bowed low
to those indifferent presences, and left.

Back in the world of time, I hungered, gasped
in the raw air of contingency, and gripped
what solace I could find, like all the rest.
But the rain-forest is with me in my dreams :
and at some moment of freedom, when I feel
the hot clasp of the body slacken, and
the steel handcuffs of necessity click apart,
I shall walk once again beneath those boughs,
and breathe the air of the place where nothing dies.

THE NIGHT-SELF CONTEMPLATES
THE ARRIVAL OF CONSCIOUSNESS

Rich blood disturbed my thought
I knew no shape nor size
I wondered, and was not:

Cradled in salt, I had
No tears to dim my eyes:
My coupled veins were glad.

Love held me cradled there:
But still I dreamed of air.

Love held me soft and coiled
O but the mind, the mind!
That tenderness was foiled:

I fed on love alone
Yet in its tender rind
My brain cried out for bone.

I writhed in my own heat:
I willed my heart to beat.

I shouldered love aside
the cold air spoke my name:
I clutched the air, and cried!

My mother's flesh lay spent,
Cool ashes after flame.
Sighing, she gave consent:

Caressed by light, I lay
Small in the human day.

Flow like milk,
stand like a table,

dance like fire,
bounce like a bed,
world of my wonderment!

milk flows over
tongue and throat,
whiteness is sweet:

table stands dark,
good to hold,
sharp to hit:

fire dances bright
and wicked!
BACK
back
to safety
mouse in a hole!

bed holds cool,
dips, waves, is
comfort to the toes.

Next, out through the door. A rippling
voyage into the bigger air. The sky
isn't a ceiling! Cool flagstones, dirt,
miracles waiting.

Get down, feel it!

Spiders watch. A world under each leaf.
Dew soaks my feet. I scramble up rough
bark. Benediction of tree and wall:
my friends that waited for me!

Not only friends.
Protection ended back there.
This world is full of sharpness. A bird
sings, then twangs and chops a worm.
Toads get squashed. My heart knots,
hard as a stone with pity. Perplexed,
a beetle kicks on his back. Won't someone help him?

Not me.
I'm afraid.

Then
the change of gear, climbing whine and scream
of the machine running faster and wilder,
its driver helpless, eyeing the dials,
his hands in his swaying lap.   Madness
stalks the arteries.   The thrush sings
in a forgotten tongue.   Who wished this trouble on me?

Difference, potent and sly, what is it they hide?
Look, it is something they carry close to themselves.
Their eyes tell of it.   But in what language?
If only I dared ask them to let me look!

Tall
the garden is full of animals
herself among them
Katya with the Kerenkas next to her thighs
an animal like the rest
tall
unfevered
as I can never be.

Now my body is made,
Now I stand in my fulness,
the road climbs always uphill.

A MURAL OF BEGGARS

then
the dream of the swart beggar in his fever,
clutching at the shape of coins.
Wrapped in newspapers
in Paris he lies on the gratings
to catch the Metro's warm
boozy breath (poxy
kiss of the bought city, cold
in her bones).
        In London or
Bombay, the beggar curses the weather
and waits.
        His eyes are
old as poverty. He has digested
the almanac of the centuries.
His patience is hard as the pavement.

We all need him. He twangs
the nerve of generosity in middling
men. Even the poor
feel rich as they decide not
to-day, to drop him a coin. But most
the rich need him, lordy! where
would the lapidary sentences of wealth
come safely to a halt, but
in the black, immovable full
stop of the empty man?

Let's appreciate : wealth makes
fine things, not for itself
alone. Even its lovely
mistakes give colour and shape
to foolishness.
        The beggar (I only

mean) is part of that
shape, and must stay
in his corner, to draw
the sight-cords tight.
                    Sansovino's
Library of San Marco, in Venice,
goes up (still pillars proud
of their balustrades! concerto for
the straight line!) watched by beggars.
The Taj Mahal swells in marble,
watched by beggars.   Grand Central
Station gathers its careful
strength into a bright knot (watched
by beggars).   All these aeronauts
take off in a blast of roubles, even
one called Valentina Something, a
woman (dainty thing!) as far
above a beggar's ravenous
dream as a *steak au
poivre*.

                    They still
break children's legs, in India
to make them grow up cripples. I
think of it when I see my own
children's new-minted air-kissing
limbs, bathed in firelight or
sunlight. Well, natch! a
beggar with no limp makes no
headway. Same thing as
an English stockbroker putting (careful
man!) his son's name for a
well-spoken-of prep. school (or
nearly the same).

                    Send flowers
to the lady astronaut! Whisk of
a powder puff round the planets!
As for the beggars,

the beggars with cold fingers,
the beggars with no shining instruments
the beggars outside Moscow railway station
the meths. drinkers on the Metro gratings
the rotting London men under the
Arches with rags stuffed into their
trousers, well,
                let them eat cake!

(*Dialogue :*
The Beggar and the Astronaut)

A. Stars drunk with their own brilliance crowd my sky.
    I hunt lost worlds, flung beyond calculation.

B. The furthest is not lonelier than I.
    Not all their maps could plot my desperation.

A. My charts and figures ring the universe.

B. I blot them with my hunger's silent curse.

A. I risk my life : does not that risk outweigh
    The cold reproaches of your life's neglect?

B. My life is mine if you toss yours away :
    I hunger still, though your swift shell lay wrecked.

A. New knowledge will not wait till you are fed.

B. Knowledge breeds knowledge : so are beggars bred.

(*Oration to all the*
beggars in the world)

      Brothers whose shivering keeps our dignity warm
      whose dangers ensure our safety like a charm

      whichever curse twists your frail bones asunder
      the panic of emptiness or the guilt of plunder

W.—D   41

we come to you at last for cure of our sickness
whose disenchanted eyes have explored our weakness

we admit now what we have always denied
what we share with you goes deeper than our pride

for want and misery lay hold of us in nightmare
our ribs are naked as yours to the whipping air

our self-sufficiency is an unconvinced parade
we are all beggars and we are all afraid

we must beg each day for the things that keep us alive
to be loved, to be needed, to walk upright, to survive

and everything goes down with the setting sun
night's forgetfulness levels all we have done

and our beggary, like yours, is endlessly renewed
in the salt deserts of our solitude

admit us therefore, we ask, into the ranks
of those whose only service is to give thanks

since our deepest needs are met only by largesse
teach us your art, brothers, to curse and bless

now is the moment when barriers collapse
admit us to your domain : we need no maps,

we are at home there, we know it well,
we have lived beside you longer than we dare tell

for beggary is our element as it is yours
the shriek of a rabbit in the eagle's claws

we are helpless before the things we have created
we have maimed what we loved, worshipped what we hated

and it is our injustice shines cold through your eyes
shaming the falsity of our vanished disguise

there can be no progress till you forgive us
and into your chaste fellowship receive us

let there be no talk of plans and fresh starts
while the world still mirrors the granite of our hearts

we confess to your helplessness and your greed
speak the word by which our chained hands may be freed

for who knows his own needs has mapped a cruel city
the roads go between walls and the wind is gritty

the most we can ask, the least we can give, is pity

The dry bone's whiteness. Shooting
green and scarlet all round, tendrils
rejoicing through the ribs. A dead man
in the rank jungle is the beggar's
emblem. And not only the beggar's. We
see this dry whiteness among rioting
fertility elsewhere: the stick of chalk
inert on the rich mould.
                              Mating,
human love, the need to touch, to hold,
the mindless pump of sex:

THE RIB

(*Sonnet:*
to Jeanne Duval)

Honey and feathers, silk of the inside lip
thick breath, hot heart, blind trembling at the knees:
her lacing fronds, his urgent slide and grip:
the sensual symphony is scored for these,

and these you gave: more still: the subtle drums,
spilt coffee on a white and starchy cloth
(through pampas grass the svelte procession comes,
the cool delicious taper claims its moth).

Only those unseen wings within him flapped
wild to be soaring in unperfumed air.
They itched beneath his skin.   He paced the room,

sick with that throbbing pain: but flew nowhere.
His naked shoulders never grew a plume.
It was his lust, not yours, that held him trapped.

Hold tight for a steep dive.   Bolt your
stomach into place, Jack.   An insanely
intrepid dive through the steep surprising
air.   Then smack into (with a plume
of spray) the salt water of our beginnings.
The bitter water that gives life.   The end
of all our dreams of coolness and purity.
But first, a climb.   Our dive starts from the
spindly ladders of a cosmic farce.

The day God slipped Adam a Mickey Finn!

Did you ever hear tell of it?
Well, Genesis is built

44

round belly-laughs but this one
is a boffo. The burlesque houses
of all time echo with that roar
of helpless laughter. Grimaldi,
Little Tich, W. C. Fields, you are
made truly after the image of God. To squirt
water from your button-hole, squelch
a custard-pie right in that sober citizen's
well-shaven jowls, that's true
piety.
              No disrespect,
I like jokes myself. They help one to face
seriousness, by coming at it sidelong.
But this was *the most!* Think of it: he's
lonely, tells the Chief he needs a girl.
It's creepy in the evenings, with no one
to answer your voice, or tell you please
to make up the stove. Eden? It's no
great draw without someone along to talk to
about how nice it is.
              So the Chief
says, Yes, all right, and then
WHAM! slips him a knock-out drop. Imagine that!

Ay, thou poor ghost, we will imagine that.
That sleep of Adam's, that thick restless swoon,
that coma hung with shadows and sharp dreams,
snakes crawling down the walls, fat spiders in
the bath (look that one up in Freud, fellows),
eyes sealed by God's occluding touch, teeth clenched,
look how his hands open and shut — he wants
to fight the beasts that attack him in his dream!
Hear him keep moaning? Adam, I would not
wish such a sleep on you.
              But that's not all!
The act gets better! What a genius, this
cosmic comedian. Out of his bag
he takes a jemmy and a silken mask.

45

A choker round his throat, a greasy cap.
He's going in for burglary! Before our eyes
he opens up the straight man's side and takes
— you'd never guess it — one of his ribs. Yes, you
heard me! I thought I'd never stop laughing. The
theatre was shaking, even the usherettes
couldn't stop watching the show. Why, I'd
go crazy if I had to watch the act
again. It was *too much*.

                 He takes this rib —
now look, ask anybody, don't believe me —
and says to him (still lying there asleep)
'You asked for it,' he says, 'you poor bastard' (or
something like that) and getting out some tools
and welding equipment, right there before our eyes
he makes it into a WOMAN!

                       Well, you can
imagine how that brought the house down. I can
still hear the way they clapped and cheered. Well, I mean!
Conjuring on top of an act like that!
'Okay,' he says, 'it's all
over', and the straight
man, Adam, gets up and takes a bow,
then all of a sudden he says 'Where's my
RIB!' and down comes his hand on that side — 'Hey!
Come back here! I'm a rib short!' Laugh? They
started again, till I thought they'd die. Honest!
I'll give him that, this Adam was quite
good in the part. I mean, he made it live.
'Where's that rib?' he says again, and 'Help!'
Just as if anybody could
help him! So of course everyone laughed
again. And *then* — just picture it! — he comes
slap face to face with this babe!

Well, after that the band just had to start
playing and the stage was cleared
for the performing seals.

What else?
A trouper knows when an act reaches its
natural finish. No one could laugh any more. I found
tears on my face. That's how hard I'd been
either laughing, or something.

Well, I *mean . . .*

(Post-operational)

His eyelids opened. Light hammered on his nerves.
The tall grass heaved, with fever or desire.
The garden rocked him with its gentle curves.

The loneliness that coiled its rusty wire
about his heart, had parted. He was free.
Love shimmered like the air above a fire.

This was the miracle that had to be.
Naked, confiding, near enough to touch,
motionless in the moving light stood she.

Was he not blest beyond analysis?
His body had no doubts: its good was here:
and, dolphin-jumping in those waves of bliss,

worshipped the moon that burned so hard and clear,
worshipped the tides that made the waters dance.
O gentle earth! O crystal atmosphere!

Yet there was fear within his avid glance.

To me it was highly comick, to see the grave Philosopher — the Rambler, —
toying with a Highland beauty! — But what could he do? He must have been
surly, and weak too, had he not behaved as he did. He would have been
laughed at, and not more respected, though less loved.

Boswell, *The Journal of a Tour to the Hebrides
with Samuel Johnson, LL.D.*, 1786.

*(The Highland Girl
contemplates Samuel Johnson)*

They sat me on his knee for a joke,
after dinner.
At first, I was afraid.

The fire was warm, and he sweated.
My body felt heavy as a pony's.

Torchlight danced on his forehead:
I wanted to touch his eyes,
They were the colour of longing.

The men raised their glasses, and laughed.
Everybody talked very loud.
I would not have been afraid to comfort him,
Had they been quiet.

He held my hand a moment, then let me go.
In the night, I woke,
roused by my own weeping.

(*Sonnet:*
Act IV, Scene iii)

'Paint till a horse may mire upon your face!'
Mad Timon screamed to those two pleasure-girls,
Raving to drown them in his own disgrace:
What did they answer? Shrug, and toss their curls?

Furs, silks, fine hangings, asses' milk, and pearls
Lying in cups of wine: a scented place
Among the cushions: spasms and cunning twirls,
The stallion member upright as a mace —

Things without words! Talk was a stink of breath.
Bodies like theirs were made to drive men mad:
What would he have them do? Scrub kitchen floors?

Years later, dying amid rags and sores,
They thought of Timon's frenzy, and were glad:
His curses warmed their blood, that cooled towards death.

THE NIGHT-SELF SEES ALL WOMEN
IN ONE WOMAN

From clay to sky
from the close-clasping
roots' tunnel to the free
fairway of starlight and openness
I trace your image,
Katya, one name for all women,
now crumpled dead on the snow
kissed to death by the cold bullets of the Twelve
and now shining moon-like full in their eyes
rising over the Twelve into the unbiddable sky
and now again sinking
settling into warmth, a nest,
close on the companionable earth:
always I trace you Katya
in many places
seeking and finding
wearing out place, time,
identity.

My need is close-knit,
earthworm-creeping, leech-lipping
and also wind-under-the-feathers
high-spiralling.

My need is fish, buffalo, piston:
and you are all.   In the tall wheat
the mouse builds a swaying house:
long tails twine for love.
Thin fish dart, but an oyster swims
slower than a tree grows:
every grace, any place is
yours.   Like printed eyes

that stare from torn paper on a hoarding
you hold my gaze. All
life is your holy mountain.

I see you now Katya
even so distant, I see you
against the black sky of threats and questions
my eyes hold you
not even a woman
not even a feminine shape
but a streak of light
red and glowing, cool and gleaming
light from a fire of comfort
or the hot coals of desire
or light from a beacon
the pale urgency of a flare
or light from the steady moon:
every kind of light has majesty
and authority, and you
have all, at all times
Katya
unknown woman of the night
of Alexander Blok
and of my clinging night

I see you there so clearly
a stripe of light
against the black
the signal of our longing, our suffering
the ecstasy of our fulfilment
and the promise of our human future
unquenchable

PRINTED BY R. & R. CLARK, LTD., EDINBURGH